LIGHTS OUT APEX

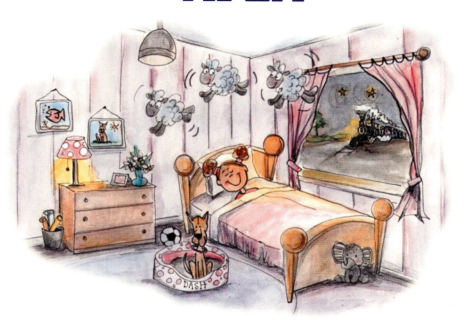

By Andrew McCauley

Illustrated by Jane Wolfgang

Text copyright © 2021 by Andrew McCauley

Illustration copyright © 2021 by Jane Wolfgang

All rights reserved.

No part of this book may be reproduced or transmitted
in any form by any means, electronic or mechanical, including photocopying,
recording, or by any information storage and retrieval system, without
permission in writing from the copyright owners.

ISBN: 978-1-7375277-0-1

Cover and Interior Layout: Debra Deysher

Printed in the United States of America
by Dash Over Books

Dedication

To my beautiful wife, Jordan, for believing in me and supporting my desire to write a children's book. Having your support is what allowed me to step out of my comfort zone and to pursue writing and publishing this book. To my daughter, Bellamy, who changed my life forever with her birth and inspired the creativity and passion needed to write this story. And to our wonderful dog, Dash, who is the star of this book and has been such a great big sister to Bellamy.

Thank you to the Apex community for welcoming my wife and I from the moment we moved here. Apex is full of friendly and genuine people, and we could not be happier with our decision to plant roots here. Thank you to all the local businesses for providing family-friendly fun, entertainment, shopping, and of course, delicious food.

Apologies to any business not included in this children's book. There are enough amazing places in Apex to write a hundred page book so we had to make some difficult decisions. I hope you and your children enjoy the book as much as I have enjoyed writing it.

Thinking of the town's past, when Log Pond was the name,
As the highest peak on the railroad, Apex it soon became.

A picture perfect town, with a future so bright,
Tomorrow will come, once we turn out the light!

The good people of Apex are ready for sleep,
It's bedtime now, start counting sheep.

Comfy and cozy so turn off the lights,
It's the "Peak Of Good Living" so say your good nights!

Rest up Common Grounds, it's time to lock your door,
Tomorrow morning there will be coffee and tea to pour.

Good night Mission Market, you offer so much to choose,
You deserve some rest now, so get home to snooze.

Nighty night tired children for the sky has turned dark,

Enjoy dreams of playing at Hunter Street Park.

Wishing a safe night to Apex firefighters and police,

Thank you for protecting and serving
to keep the peace.

Lights out
 Salem Street Pub,
you've left
 us well fed,

Dreams of delicious burgers dancing in our head.

So long
    Apex Nature Park,
        where it is
            never boring,

A long day of hiking and you will end up snoring.

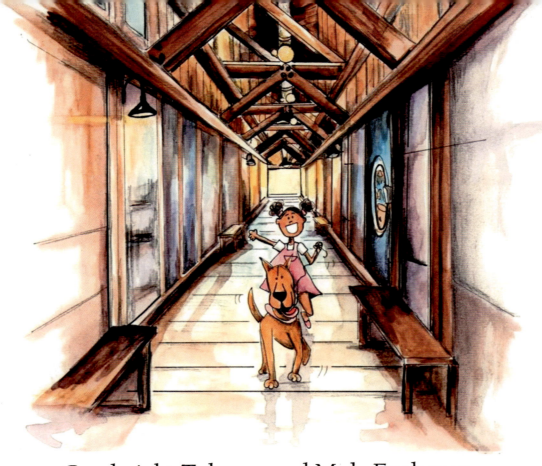

Good night Tobacco and Mule Exchange,
a building from days of old,

The morning will bring opportunities for much more to be sold.

Sweet dreams Anna's, put away the sauce and cheese,

The people are FULL

and ready to catch some ZZZZZZZ'S.

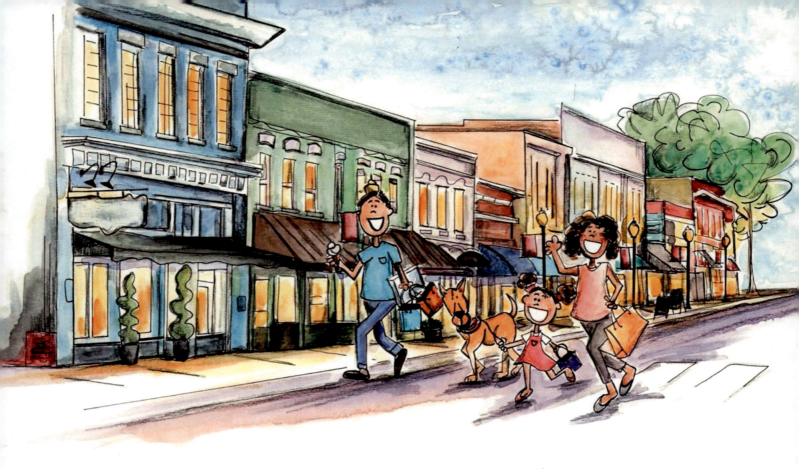

See you tomorrow busy shops on Salem Street,

Shop owners are heading home to rest their tired feet.

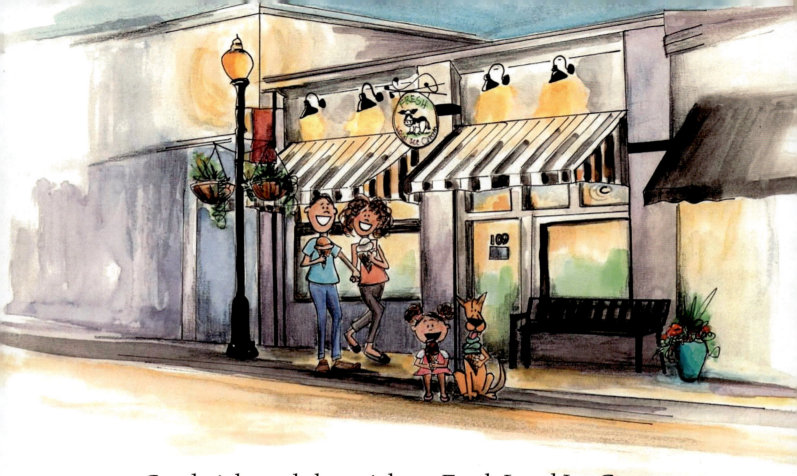

Good night and sleep tight to Fresh Local Ice Cream,

Lots of YUMMY FLAVORS give us all SWEET DREAMS.

Water
   tower bright,
      train chugging
   down the tracks,

Head on your pillow, close your eyes and relax.

In a few short moments you will run out of sheep,
Dreaming of Apex living, it's the Peak of good sleep.

Good night to Apex and all of our friends,
For tomorrow night when we shall do it all again!

Have **YOU** been everywhere **DASH** has been?

If you've gone **EVERYWHERE**, then just go **AGAIN**!

Mission Market

Common Grounds

Hunter Street Park

Salem Street Pub

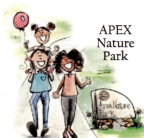
APEX Nature Park

Tobacco and Mule Exchange

Fresh Local Ice Cream

Shops on Salem Street

Anna's Pizzeria

Facebook Scavenger Hunt

Explore Dash's favorite places in person if you live in Apex or in reading the book, and mark where you've been on your own scavenger hunt.

Hang it on your wall and let Dash bring you **SWEET DREAMS** of your favorite places!

Download and print the scavenger hunt page at:

Dash Over Books

About the Author

Andrew is a native of Buffalo, NY who moved to Apex with his wife, Jordan, in the Fall of 2018. Andrew always enjoyed creative writing as a child and had his passion sparked by the birth of his daughter, Bellamy, in September of 2020.

Andrew looks forward to writing additional children's books in the future.

Email: dashoverbooks@gmail.com
Facebook: Dash Over Books

About the Illustrator

Jane is a retired art teacher from York, PA who fell in love with the town of Apex, NC while living there. She is an accomplished artist who works in many mediums and she continues to teach classes and workshops.

This is Jane's ninth illustrated children's book.

You can follow Jane and her work at www.Janewolfgang.com or on social media @janewolfgangart.

Made in the USA
Columbia, SC
12 August 2021

42798510R00022